Green in Gray
The Art of Adaptability in Urban Agriculture

Table of Contents

Chapter 1. Introduction

Immerse yourself in "Green in Gray: The Art of Adaptability in Urban Agriculture," a special report that brings the vibrancy and vitality of nature right into the heart of urban living. This fascinating read fuses the scientific, with the practical, and the artful, and seeks to carve a clear path toward sustainability in even the most concrete-laden landscapes. From rooftops to basements, discover the innovative methods and inspiring tales of urban farming triumphs that are fundamentally changing the way we see our cities. As you delve into this special report, you will feel the energy and optimism of a greener future, and you too may be drawn into the urban farming revolution. Don't wait, secure your copy today, and let the transformation of gray to green commence!

Chapter 2. The Green Revolution: Start of Urban Agriculture

From pastures and plowed fields, agriculture seems an unlikely candidate for urbanization. Yet a radical transformation is taking place that redefines the connection between food and the urban environment. This development, known as urban agriculture, coalesces around the concept of sustainability, food security, community engagement, and environmental stewardship.

2.1. Historical Context

Urban agriculture is far from a novelty. In wartime and depression, urbanites have traditionally turned to their backyards, balconies, and vacant lots as sources of fresh food. In America during World War II, homeowners cultivated Victory Gardens that produced a remarkable 40% of the nation's fresh produce.

Though urban farming waned with post-war prosperity, the seeds of change, once sown, never fully retreat. Modern urban agriculture, in many ways, is an echo of these resilient Victory Gardens, revitalized by the urgency of contemporary environmental and social challenges.

2.2. The Emergence of Urban Agriculture

Often catalyzed by financial crises, food shortages, and a growing awareness of the environmental impact of conventional farming practices, urban agriculture has gained momentum in the last few decades.

In Cuba during the "Special Period" in the 1990s, when the nation faced famine-like conditions following the Soviet Union's collapse, urban agriculture emerged organically as a survival strategy. Today, this island nation is a model for urban organic farming, with more than 385,000 urban farms spreading oasis-like across its cityscapes.

The advocacy for local, organic, and sustainable food systems also accelerated the urban agriculture movement in North America and Europe. Today, the scope of urban agriculture is expansive - from community gardens to corporate rooftops, hydroponics to mushroom cultivation in disused subway tunnels.

2.3. Urban Agriculture Methods

Urban agriculture relies on innovative and adaptable practices to compensate for space limitations and soil contamination issues. Here are some of the most prevalent methods:

- Raised Bed Gardening: Cultivates crops in substantial wooden frames filled with high-quality soil.

- Hydroponics: Grows plants in nutrient-rich solutions, eliminating soil altogether.

- Aquaponics: Combines aquaculture (raising aquatic organisms like fish) with hydroponics in symbiotic environments.

- Vertical Farming: Uses layered, often tiered structures for cultivation.

Each system offers unique advantages, often combining various methods to maximize space, resource efficiency, and yield.

2.4. The Promise of Urban Agriculture

By producing food nearer to where it's consumed, urban agriculture reduces "food miles." In turn, this substitution to long transportation chains shrinks associated greenhouse gas emissions. Urban agriculture's localization also promotes food security, offering city dwellers improved access to fresh produce.

It creates green spaces and improves urban biodiversity. Self-evidently, so-called "concrete jungles" become more pleasant, healthier environments, thanks to urban agriculture.

Urban farming also holds social benefits. Many initiatives focus on community engagement to tackle issues like social isolation, offering communal spaces that foster relationships and wellbeing. Education about nutrition and food production is another crucial facet of urban agriculture.

2.5. Challenges and the Road Ahead

However, hurdles remain. Land access, soil contamination, and inadequate investment are some constraints urban farmers face. Still, progressive urban planning policies, combined with innovative technological developments, may well prove pivotal in resolving such issues.

Urban agriculture, as part of an integrated approach to urban resilience, reveals the potential for cities as agents of environmental change. As the global population urbanizes, the challenge and indeed, the necessity to integrate nature into urban life becomes more acute. Urban agriculture is a compelling answer to this call, uniting the arcadian and the metropolitan in an innovative, verdant harmony.

In conclusion, the rise of urban agriculture marks a significant shift in our understanding of sustainable food systems. It blends green elements harmoniously within the gray urban landscapes, transforming them into thriving hubs of life and community. It reacquaints the urban with the rural, bringing us one step closer to a greener, more sustainable future. And so, the green revolution continues, growing ever stronger in each urban plot, rooftop garden, and basement aquaponic system amidst our cityscapes.

Chapter 3. The Necessary Shift: Understanding Urban Agriculture Needs

In a world where populous urban centers dominate the landscape, there is a compelling need for us to critically rethink and transform the way we approach agriculture. Far removed from the bucolic imagery of verdant pastures, urban agriculture wields the power to redefine the connotations of urban living and bring us a step closer to achieving an equitable and sustainable future.

3.1. Defining Urban Agriculture

Urban agriculture refers to the cultivation, processing, and distribution of food and other products through plant cultivation and seldom, animal husbandry, within and around cities. It encompasses a broad spectrum of activities ranging from subsistence farming and small-scale gardening to the cultivation of vacant urban lands and commercial enterprises. Whichever form it takes, it invariably contributes to food security, fosters community resilience, and cultivates a sense of place and belonging among urban dwellers.

3.2. The Current Need for Urban Agriculture

It's important not to overlook the critical need for urban agriculture in contemporary society. As of now, over 55% of the world's population resides in urban areas, a figure projected to rise to 68% by 2050, according to the United Nations. This exponential rush towards urban living creates a litany of challenges, key amongst them being the problem of food security. Urban dwellers are highly prone to food insecurity due to the escalating cost of living, geographical remoteness from rural farms, and lack of access to fresh produce.

The resiliency of the urban food system is another growing concern. Globalization and intensified agricultural practices have turned food systems into complex webs that span vast geographies. While these systems ensure a continuous food flow, they exhibit a high level of vulnerability to shocks such as disease outbreaks, natural disasters, and fluctuations in global markets. Urban agriculture can effectively mitigate these issues through localized food production, reducing the dependency on unstable global supply chains.

Furthermore, the environmental benefits of urban agriculture can not be overstated. Urban farming practices can serve as carbon sinks, reducing greenhouse gas emissions by sequestering carbon dioxide. Growing food in cities also reduces the transport requirements for food delivery, cutting down on fuel use and emissions. At the same time, urban farming generates bio-waste that can be used as compost, diverting waste from landfills and contributing to a closed-loop urban ecosystem.

3.3. Adoption Hurdles and Potential Solutions

Despite its manifold benefits, urban agriculture faces numerous hurdles in its path of widespread adoption. Key among these are land scarcity, soil contamination, high startup costs, and regulatory restrictions. Even the best-intended urban agriculture initiatives can fizzle out without appropriate support systems and a favorable policy environment in place.

However, there are tangible solutions to these hurdles. Innovative farming methods, such as vertical aeroponic farming and hydroponics, can circumvent the issue of land scarcity, turning even a small rooftop or basement into a green oasis. Local governments play a crucial role in remedying soil contamination through regulations, guidelines, and remediation programs - these need to be further strengthened and systematically implemented. High startup costs can be offset by financial grants, micro-loans, and training opportunities for aspiring urban farmers provided by the community, city councils, or non-profit organizations. Last but not least, regulatory restrictions need systematic dismantlement, and local governments must establish urban agriculture-friendly policies, from zoning laws to tax rebates.

3.4. Moving Forward: The Future of Urban Agriculture

Looking ahead, the future of urban agriculture resides in our hands. The need for it has never been more imperative and pressing. Integrating urban farming into our societal fabric will require a complete paradigm shift. Local governments, communities, and urban dwellers need to work hand-in-hand to foster this adaptation, paving the way for more resilient, sustainable, and equitable urban landscapes.

As we continue to push the boundary of what a city can be, we must ensure that we keep our connection with nature alive. Urban agriculture offers a solid pathway towards this goal. The integration of green amidst the gray extends far beyond the physical transformation of spaces - it represents the much-needed shift in mindset about how life in the modern urban environment can and should be. Only by realizing this necessity and embracing the shift, can a greener, more sustainable and resilient urban future become a tangible reality.

With each seed sown, each plant nurtured, and each harvest reaped within the heart of our cities, we draw a line in the concrete, creating a clear path, a verdant trail towards a sustainable urban future. And in doing so, we make a collective statement - a statement of resilience, adaptation, community, and hope for the future. As we nurture the green within the gray, we're not merely transforming cityscapes. We're reshaping our futures, one garden, one rooftop, one vacant lot at a time.

Chapter 4. Sky-high Crops: An Introduction to Rooftop Farming

Unveiling the urban skyline to a new realm of possibilities where the barren terraces of high-rise buildings become lush green farmland, rooftop farming emerges as the resilient reply from nature lovers, urban farmers, and sustainability advocates confronted with the gray, often monochromatic character of sprawling metropolises. As one delves deeper into this captivating world of airborne cultivation, it becomes evident that rooftop farming offers more than just a pleasant splash of verdant shades against the austere cityscape. This innovative farming method is redefining our interaction with nature in matrixed urban settings while reshaping our approach to sustainable living.

4.1. The Fundamental Concept: Sowing Seeds atop Concrete Pillars

The concept of rooftop farming, at its core, involves the utilization of rooftop spaces - a seemingly underused city resource - to cultivate a wide diversity of crops. This often entails transforming concrete roofs into green habitats where fruits, vegetables, herbs, and even smaller livestock thrive. Urban landscapes, notoriously encumbered with spatial constraints, geographical impediments, and environmental challenges, are thus offered unexpected shots at self-sustainability, food security, and ecosystem restoration.

4.2. A Brief Foray into Rooftop Farming History

Rooftop farming is not an entirely new discipline. The Hanging Gardens of Babylon, one of the seven wonders of the ancient world, is arguably the earliest known evidence of vertical, aerial farming. However, modern-day rooftop farming, with its strong ties to sustainable urbanism, came to prominence as a mainstream practice around the 1960s in Germany. The idea quickly spread across Europe, later gaining traction in North American countries as an effective method to counter urban food insecurity, reduce the carbon footprint of cities, and enhance biodiversity.

4.3. The Context: Why Rooftop Farming Matters

In a world scorched by environmental degradation and spiraling urbanization, rooftop farming emerges as a robust solution now, more than ever. Rooftop farms provide a productive use for otherwise wasted space and buoy up urban food supply chains, increasing local food production. This not only cuts down food miles but also results in fresher fare landing on urban diners' plates.

Furthermore, these aerial farms curtail stormwater runoff, decrease the urban heat island effect, increase citywide biodiversity, and sequester carbon. The positive impact on mental health born from increased green vistas in a cityscape cannot be overlooked either, along with the strengthening sense of community and connectivity such initiatives inspire.

4.4. The Mechanics: Cultivating Crops in the Sky

Rooftop farming can take several forms, ranging from container gardening to installing green roofs, aquaponics, and even sophisticated, fully-fledged hydroponic systems. The choice of method largely depends on the specific constraints and possibilities each building entails, including roof stability, waterproofing and access conditions, and the potential for sun and rainwater collection.

Rooftop farming's high dependence on efficient water management implies that rainwater harvesting features prominently in most arrangements. The harvested water, stored in on-site tanks, used in concert with drip irrigation systems, ensures low water consumption. Solar power installations are also popular among rooftop farmers, presenting a sustainable energy source for all essential agricultural operations.

Despite the sense of novelty surrounding rooftop farming, the basic principles at play are much akin to conventional agriculture. Seasonal cycles of planting, growing, harvesting, and resting the soil are observed, while crop rotation and companion planting feature prominently to promote soil health and prevent maladies.

4.5. The Challenges: Hurdles Along the Green Path

Rooftop farming is not without its unique set of challenges. The start-up cost, ensuring structural safety, arranging access, managing soil and water supplies, and navigating local regulations around the use and alteration of rooftops can pose significant difficulties for aspiring rooftop farmers. Moreover, achieving optimal crop yield and health in the middle of an urban heat island can demand meticulous planning, constant monitoring, and appropriate contingencies.

4.6. From Gray to Green: Case Studies of Success

Several cities across the globe serve as living testaments to rooftop farming's transformative potential. From New York's Brooklyn Grange, the world's largest rooftop soil farm, to Hong Kong's Rooftop Republic, where more than 60 rooftop farms have been set up over just a few years, these thriving projects exhibit a promising trajectory toward urban self sufficiency in food production, and a more harmonious cohabitation with nature.

4.7. A Glimmering Horizon: The Future of Rooftop Farming

With the alarming pitfalls of climate change becoming ever more apparent, and the incessant churn of urbanization creeping ahead, the need for sustainable food production modes that coexist within the urban fabric has never been more critical.

As technology makes strides in precision agriculture, planning and managing rooftop farms with the help of remote sensing, soil sensors, and AI-based prediction models will likely become commonplace. The symbiosis of technology and rooftop farming could well lead to the rise of autonomous 'smart' rooftop farms capable of optimizing their own watering, nutrition deployment, pest control, and harvesting schedules.

In the realm of regulations and policies, supportive regulatory frameworks and financial incentives will play a key role in promoting rooftop farming. With cities like Toronto, San Francisco, and Copenhagen, already mandating green roofs in new buildings, we can anticipate an increasing wave of such support in the not-so-distant future.

Rooftop farming, the novel art of taming the urban sky, is quickly moving from being a niche novelty and taking its honorable place within the sustainable agriculture mainstream. This transformation of the grayscale rooftops to prolific green landscapes yields more than a visual spectacle. It is a strong statement, a calculated rebellion, an undeniable affirmation of our latent potential to fuse the seemingly dissonant realms of the steel city and the nurturing soil, crafting sanctuaries of sustainability and resilience that soar high above the concrete sprawl.

Chapter 5. Concrete Jungles: The Edible Landscape Movement

Imagine an urban expanse of asphalt and gray slabs of concrete, punctuated by tall buildings, where the sun's rays are intercepted by windowpanes rather than absorbed by green leaves. This is not an environment that brings to mind thoughts of nature's bounty or cultivation. But a revolution is sweeping these seemingly inhospitable landscapes, harnessing the power of human ingenuity to turn concrete jungles into thriving oases of sustainable produce - right at the heart of the city. Welcome to the Edible Landscape Movement.

5.1. The Genesis of the Movement

Historically, rural areas have been the primary source of food production. The sprawling fields, breezy orchards, and vast pastures seemed the natural and only suitable habitats for agriculture. Then came urbanization, and with it, challenges to this agrarian norm. Urban expansion brought about the displacement of green spaces, fragmenting ecosystems, and altering the delicate balance of biodiversity. Yet, it is within this very urban sprawl that the solutions to these challenges have started to emerge. The Edible Landscape Movement is one such solution.

The Movement began as a simple, pragmatic response to limited local food sourcing opportunities in urbanized areas. It was a recognition that urban dwellers constitute a significant (and growing) portion of the world's population and that they too deserve access to fresh, local produce. Eventually, however, the Movement evolved and expanded in scope, advocating for more than just local food. It represents a transformative shift in the way we perceive and use urban spaces.

5.2. Unearthling the Potential

At its core, the Edible Landscape Movement seeks to re-imagine and re-engineer urban spaces for primary food production. It aims to unlock the productive potential lying dormant beneath layers of concrete, converting spaces traditionally seen as barren into functioning ecosystems teeming with edible plants.

Community gardens, rooftop farms, and even subsurface farming in city basements are emerging, quite literally, from the ground up. In each case, the ambition remains universal: to transform the urban landscape from a consumer of resources into a regenerative and sustaining environment.

This potential extends to more than just food production. It encompasses other ecosystem services, such as local climate regulation, air purification, and support for urban wildlife. It thereby broadens the implications of urban farming beyond the realm of agriculture, linking it with other environmental goals and urban planning objectives.

5.3. The Big Picture: Developing an Ecosystem

Edible landscapes are more than a collection of individual gardens and farms. They are cultivated networks, interconnected in ways traditional farming landscapes often are not. Gardens and farms within an urban area can be linked in a closed-loop system, where waste from one site becomes a resource for another, and where a ripple effect of benefits is felt far beyond the farm gate.

To achieve this, the edible landscape movement employs principles from fields as diverse as permaculture, agroecology, and urban planning. It borrows strategies from nature to make farming operations more resilient, efficient, and sustainable. For example, planting polycultures (combining different plant species in the same area) increases biodiversity and resilience, while composting converts organic waste into high-value soil amendments.

5.4. Breaking New Ground: Success Stories

The Edible Landscape Movement is far from a pipe dream; it's already yielding impressive results. In New York City, an organization called Brooklyn Grange manages over 5.6 acres of rooftop farms, yielding more than 50,000 lbs of organically-cultivated produce each year. In Tokyo, Pasona O2 is revitalizing the city's subterranean spaces for hydroponic farming, reaping harvests beneath the city's bustling surface.

In Cuba, Havana's organoponicos, or urban organic gardens, produce over 60% of the fruits and vegetables consumed in the city. And in Singapore, the urban farm Sky Greens has maximized skyward growth with its vertical farming technology.

5.5. From Idea to Implementation: Key Prerequisites

There are challenges to cultivating edible landscapes in concrete jungles. The space, light, and soil requirements for food crops can be difficult to meet in built-up urban areas. Zoning regulations, policy limitations, capital constraints, and knowledge gaps can also present hurdles.

Balancing these challenges requires careful planning, innovative thinking, and often, policy support. Advocacy, education, community engagement, and integrated land use planning are key tools in the edible landscape movement's toolkit that can help overcome these obstacles. Moreover, urban farmers must constantly adapt their practices to space, light, and soil constraints, often requiring creative and highly specialized growing methods.

5.6. The Future: Sagacity and Sustainability

The continuing urbanization of our world underscores the increasing urgency for urban agriculture. By integrating food production, ecosystem services, and urban planning principles, the Edible Landscape Movement offers more than just solution—it acts as a beacon, guiding our cities towards a greener, healthier, and more sustainable future.

Indeed, the Edible Landscape Movement is not merely a means to feed our urban populations. It is an instrument of transformation, an inspiration, and a demonstration of the potential for human ingenuity to adapt and thrive in any environment. We may have created our cities as concrete jungles, but with some wisdom and vision, we can cultivate them into concrete gardens. The promise of the Edible Landscape Movement lies not just in its harvests, but also in its power to change our way of life, our relationships with nature, and perhaps even, our understanding of what a city can be.

Chapter 6. Community Gardens: Seeds of Social Change and Sustainability

In the heart of sprawling urban jungles, communities are reclaiming forgotten corners and derelict lots, transforming them into verdant havens of fruit, vegetable, and newfound social cohesion. Community gardens represent a bridge between the past and the future: an incorporation of ancestral agricultural practices paired with innovative farming techniques to address pressing social, environmental, and health dilemmas within the urban fabric.

6.1. A Historical Perspective

The emergence of community gardens as we know them today is a relatively recent phenomenon, largely influenced by prevailing societal needs and conditions. A brief look into history reveals this trend.

During World War I and II, the government sponsored Victory Gardens to boost food production and morale on the home front. These gardens, which were mostly in rural and suburban areas, re-emerged in cities during the 1970s and 80s as a response to urban decay and increasing food insecurity. They evolved into community gardens, fostering not only food production but also social bonds among disparate urban dwellers.

6.2. The Multifaceted Benefits of Urban Agriculture

Community gardens generate a cornucopia of benefits, some tangible and quantifiable, others less so, but no less critical.

The most obvious advantage lies in food production. Urban gardens usually follow organic principles, yielding fresh, local, and highly nutritious foods. This direct supply mitigates the influence of industrial agriculture, reduces food miles, and offers an antidote to the food deserts that plague many cities.

However, food production constitutes merely a fraction of what community gardens contribute. These pockets of green in gray landscapes act as oxygen factories, absorbing carbon dioxide and other pollutants while recharging the city's air quality. They provide habitat for local wildlife, increasing the city's biodiversity. Most importantly, community gardens transform idle, underutilized spaces into verdant and productive landscapes - a step toward combating urban heat island effect.

6.3. Social Cohesion and Cultural Exchange

More than spaces for growing food, community gardens are instrumental in sowing seeds of social change. They are platforms for cultural exchange and education. Each garden plot becomes a symbol of the gardener's roots, a testament to his or her relationship with nature, often reflected through the choice of crops.

Moreover, community gardens can foster stronger neighborhoods. When people of different backgrounds come together to till the soil, cross-pollination of ideas, knowledge, and camaraderie happens. This sense of shared purpose often extends beyond the perimeter of the garden, encouraging community development and cooperation.

6.4. Urban Gardens as Learning Laboratories

Teaching future generations about nature can be a challenge amidst skyscrapers' shadows. Community gardens offer real-life laboratories where children and adults alike can interact with nature and learn about the cycles of life.

Within its natural classroom, a community garden shares lessons in sustainability and ecology, nutrition, and even business and commerce, as some gardens encourage selling surplus produce at local markets. The practical, hands-on learning in these gardens can supplement traditional education methods and foster a new generation of urban farmers.

6.5. Combating Food Insecurity

In the face of increasing food insecurity in cities, community gardens can provide much-needed relief. They can step in where commercial outlets are unwilling or unable to operate, providing fresh, nutritious, and accessible produce locally. The sustainable practices ingrained in community gardens can cultivate self-reliance and resilience in urban communities, helping to break the cycle of food poverty.

6.6. Conclusion

The complexity and urgency of contemporary urban challenges necessitate innovative and multifaceted solutions. Community gardens rise to this call, addressing environmental, social, and health objectives while transitioning our concrete jungles towards more green, resilient, and sustainable models.

Enabling this transition requires bolstering supportive policy frameworks, promoting community participation, and investing in educational initiatives. The vibrant beetroots of these gardens are symbols of resistance and resilience, reminders of our symbiosis with nature, even within the heart of our cities.

In this era of concrete and glass, community gardens stand testament to the power of green, demonstrating that every seed sown is not simply an act of cultivation, but a conscious step towards social change and sustainability.

Chapter 7. From Waste to Bounty: Composting and Urban Soil Management

Cities produce vast amounts of waste. Instead of paying to haul it away, or worse, dumping it into landfills, the organic fraction can be turned into a valuable resource. This is where composting comes into play, a process that diverts waste from urban sprawl and serves a critical role in maintaining the soil's health.

7.1. The Essentials of Composting

In essence, composting is nature's way of recycling. Composting at a fundamental level is a process where organic materials like garden waste, food scraps, and paper products are broken down by earth's little workers – microorganisms. The heroes of this aerobic process, paired with controlled moisture, temperature, and aeration, result in a nutrient-rich amendment that enhances the soil's fertility and structure.

7.2. Different Techniques of Urban Composting

There are a variety of methods to compost effectively in an urban environment, based on space availability, organic material resources, and desired composting speed. These techniques include vermicomposting, bokashi, trench composting, and stackable compost bins.

Vermicomposting utilizes worms (usually red wigglers) to consume organic waste and produce castings, a rich soil amendment. Bokashi composting relies on specific microbial communities to ferment waste in a sealed container. Trench composting directly integrates green waste into the soil.

Choose the technique that fits your urban spaces, time constraints, and type of waste you generate.

7.3. Addressing Urban Composting Challenges

The urban landscape provides unique challenges to composting, including space constraints, potential odors, attracting pests, and managing variable inputs of waste. Composting can be successful by experimenting with different methods, continually monitoring, adjusting as needed, and communicating with neighbors and the community.

7.4. Soil Management as Part of Urban Agriculture

Soil management is a crucial aspect of urban agriculture. Ensuring balanced levels of nutrients is vital for healthy plant growth and high-quality produce. From analyzing soil composition to implementing compost and other organic supplements, urban farmers have much to consider.

7.5. Soil Analysis for Optimal Crop Health

Soil testing gives the composition of your soil - its structure, pH value, and nutrient content. This information is key to determining what changes are needed to optimize the soil environment for different crops.

7.6. Role of Compost in Urban Soil Management

Composting closes the loop of organic waste, recycling it back into the soil as a rich amendment. Compost improves soil structure, releases nutrients slowly, retains moisture, and helps suppress diseases. It is an affordable and sustainable strategy for urban soil management.

7.7. The Promise of Composting for Urban Agriculture

As cities expand and populous increase, the need for local food production is inevitable. Urban agriculture mitigates food insecurity, improves community health, and can play an integral part of urban sustainability through waste reduction. The promise of compost, as a product of such waste, is undeniable.

Whether it's a high-rise rooftop farm or a backyard garden, shifting from waste to bounty will take concerted effort, but it is within our reach. The triple bottom line of composting—people (urban farmers and community), profit (sale of compost and savings in waste disposal), and planet (reduced landfill waste and carbon emissions)—can effectively interweave with urban agricultural systems.

This chapter has covered the basic principles of composting, explored different composting methods suitable for urban settings, discussed hurdles and their potential solutions, and delved into the significance of effective soil management and composting's role in it. Through composting, with its numerous environmental, economic, and social benefits, we can seize the opportunity to turn waste into a treasure—a bounty of nutrition for the urban soil that will support the growth of healthy and sustainable cities.

Chapter 8. Aquaponics and Hydroponics: Water Wise Food Production Systems

Aquaponics and hydroponics are two revolutionary strategies that exhibit the potential of urban farming. Both methods defy the conventional perceptions of agriculture, creating thriving environments for plant and aquatic growth in non-traditional spaces. Neither of these techniques requires soil, an element often scarce in urban spaces, which makes them perfect contenders for inner-city food production. While aquaponics presents a symbiotic relationship between aquaculture and hydroponics, hydroponics provides a unique solution that entirely hinges on water usage. Let's explore these two strategies in depth.

8.1. A Dive into Hydroponics

Hydroponics is a subset of hydroculture and employs nutrient-rich water as the primary source for plant anatomy, eliminating the necessity for soil. Here, plants extract their required nutrients directly from the water, which can be routinely refreshed to maintain balance.

8.1.1. The Birth of Hydroponics

The idea of hydroponics isn't an avant-garde concept. Ancient civilizations like the Egyptians, Aztecs, and the people of the Hanging Gardens of Babylon were already aware of this agricultural methodology. But the elucidation of plant nutrition and subsequent development of nutrient solutions in the 19th and 20th century brought hydroponics in the contemporary sense to the forefront.

8.1.2. Nutrient Solution: The Lifeblood of Hydroponics

The nutrient solution is the crux of a hydroponic system. It is a water-based, carefully curated mix containing macronutrients like Nitrogen, Phosphorus, and Potassium, and micronutrients like Iron, Manganese, and Zinc. Analytical tools like Electrical Conductivity (EC) meters or titration kits are used to monitor the nutrient levels.

8.1.3. Systems of Hydroponics

There's an array of diversified designs for hydroponic systems, each with their strengths and challenges. The choice of system often depends on the type of crop, the availability of resources, as well as the farmer's expertise. DWC (Deep Water Culture), NFT (Nutrient Film Technique), and Ebb and Flow systems are some of the most prevalent variants.

8.2. The World of Aquaponics

Aquaponics combines the practice of hydroponics with aquaculture, the breeding, rearing, and harvesting of aquatic organisms in controlled environments. This symbiotic system accentuates the benefits of both methods while mitigating their limitations.

8.2.1. Symbiosis in Aquaponics

Aquaponics mimics nature's cycle where waste from the fish provides essential nutrients for the plants, which in turn, purify the water for fish. This symbiosis creates a closed, sustainable ecosystem with significantly lower water and nutrient requirements than hydroponics.

8.2.2. Biofilter: The Pillar of Aquaponics

A biofilter, sometimes referred to as grow bed, is the nexus that interlinks the aquatic and plant components of an aquaponics system. It houses beneficial bacteria that break down the fish waste, converting the by-products into nutrients that plants can assimilate.

8.2.3. Scaling Aquaponics

From small-scale home systems to commercial production facilities, aquaponics is highly scalable. Small-scale systems typically feature ornamental fish like goldfish or betta, while commercial-scale operations may use tilapia or barramundi that offer additional economic benefits.

8.3. Choosing Between Aquaponics and Hydroponics

Both systems offer unique advantages. Hydroponics can achieve higher yields with lower investment costs, but they require careful management of nutrient solutions. Conversely, aquaponics setups require less labor due to their symbiotic nature but require greater initial investments and expertise in managing both fish and plants.

8.4. Final Words

Urban agriculture faces unprecedented challenges. Scarce space, high infrastructure costs, fluctuating weather conditions, intense resource competition, and many more. However, with innovative methods such as hydroponics and aquaponics, we are slowly but steadily overcoming these challenges, paving the way for a greener future. These revolutionary methods are redefining our views on agriculture, offering a glimmer of hope in maneuvering through the concrete jungle towards the ultimate goal of sustainability.

Chapter 9. The Urban Apiary: Honeybees in the City

Beginning with a rather intrepid sort of ethos, urban beekeeping is a critical venture within urban agriculture. While traditionally, the notion of keeping bees is associated with bucolic country settings, the truth is far more dynamic. Cities, with their expanses of biodiversity are becoming premier locations for beekeeping, tucking apiaries in the unlikeliest of spaces. From rooftop hives overlooking bustling streets to miniature apiaries situated in park corners, urban beekeeping is responsible for initiating a profound transformation in our interaction with and understanding of nature.

9.1. Urban Bees Vs Rural Bees

A popular misconception among many is that cities are no place for bees, primarily due to the limited flora compared to the countryside. A 2015 study dissects this myth by establishing the fact that urban bees are more productive than their rural counterparts. Urban bees enjoy a diverse diet given the variety of ornamental plants and trees found within city parks, gardens and boulevards, which bloom at varying intervals across the year. Moreover, city settings are free from commercial farming pesticides, eliminating the risk of related illnesses in bees.

9.2. From Grey Rooftops to Buzzing Hubs

Concrete rooftops, seemingly barren and inhospitable, are being transformed into buzzing oases teeming with life. These greener spaces in the sky offer several advantages over flat land honey farms. Elevated from ground nuisances like pedestrians, pests, pets, or even vandals, rooftops serve as an ideal setting for honeybee colonies.

Another unexpected benefit arises from the urban heat island effect. Cities are often several degrees warmer than the surrounding areas thanks to the absorption and release of heat from buildings and asphalt. This aspect allows urban bees to forage for longer periods as cooler weather activities are pushed later into the fall.

9.3. The Making of an Urban Beekeeper

Urban beekeeping isn't simply a matter of installing a hive on a rooftop and waiting for honey. It's a practice that demands commitment and knowledge. Potential beekeepers will need both theoretical knowledge about bee behavior and hive structure, and practical skills involving the maintenance of hives and prevention of diseases.

Tools-of-the-trade include the hive, hive tools, a smoker, which pacifies the bees during hive inspections, and safety equipment such as bee suits and gloves. Moreover, it's vital to secure required permissions and adhere to local regulations for keeping bees in an urban environment.

9.4. The Fringe Benefits: More Than Just Honey

While an obvious boon of urban beekeeping is honey, it's by no means the only advantage. Bees play a vital role in pollinating plants, that leads to the production of fruits, vegetables, and nuts. Without bees, you say goodbye to almonds, peaches, and a multitude of other beloved foods. Urban beekeeping, thus, enables the transformation of urban green spaces into blossoming fruit and vegetable gardens.

Moreover, bees offer a lesson in sustainability. From the structure of their hives, which optimizes space through hexagonal cells, to a strict no-waste policy, where every element of the hive is allocated a staid purpose, the sting of the bee carries the echo of a greener urban future.

9.5. Dealing With Potential Challenges

Existing amidst the clamor and humdrum of city life, urban beekeeping has to deal with its unique set of challenges. Urban noise and pollution could potentially harm the bees, necessitating hive sites to be carefully selected. Other challenges involve managing hive health proactively to prevent against different bee diseases, and even understanding swarm behavior to effectively control and settle them without causing panic among nearby residents.

Facing these challenges directly and devising dynamic solutions around them is fundamental to seamlessly integrating beekeeping into the urban fabric.

9.6. Conclusion

Urban apiculture is not a passing fad; it's a solid manifestation of the urban desire to reconnect with nature and choose sustainable alternatives. As cities expand, the fate of our food, health, and climate are intertwined with the humble honeybee. Promoting urban beekeeping is an essential step towards making our cities more sustainable, liveable, and more resilient. By cultivating a symbiotic relationship with these industrious insects, cities provide not only a haven for the bees— they foster a more harmonious, smarter urban ecosystem, indicative of the transformative power of urban agriculture. It's truly, where the grey meets the green.

Chapter 10. Revolutionizing Urban Livestock: Chicken, Goats, and Beyond

Starting with what many think of as the traditional farmyard, let's consider livestock—the chicken and the goat. These animals have found their way onto rooftops and into backyards in metropolitan areas worldwide, proving that our visions of farming must extend beyond the traditional rural setting.

10.1. A New Coop in Town: Urban Chickens

In the heart of ever-rumbling city traffic, chickens scratch, cluck, and lay their eggs. Chickens, being compact, personable, and productive, seem built for urban farming. Many city dwellers find the allure of fresh eggs irresistible. The hassle of having to weave through overly crowded supermarket aisles to select a carton of eggs that came from thousands of miles away steadily loses allure when compared to 'hyper-local' eggs.

The trend of urban chicken keeping has not only been boosted by the desire for fresh produce but by a rejuvenation in the nature-human connection. Studies have shown that chickens exhibit a wide range of behaviors, emotions, and personalities, furthering their fame in the city farming narrative as more than just egg-laying machines.

10.2. Pioneering the Farm-to-Table Approach

Urban chicken raising is seen as pioneering the farm-to-table philosophy in the city. Caring for hens provides not only a rich learning experience but also contributes to a sustainable lifestyle by transforming kitchen waste into compost through chicken feed. This cyclical approach helps reduce waste and enhances the productivity of urban kitchen gardens.

However, the urban setting does bring some challenges. Local zoning regulations might limit the number of roosters or hens you can keep, while potential health concerns should be managed carefully through regular checkups and vaccinations (for instance against Avian Influenza).

10.3. Goat: A Sustainable Icon for Urban Agriculture

The trend of urban goats is largely spurred by the desire for fresh, local dairy produce. Not just for milk, goats also provide cheese, yogurt, soap, and even fiber for spinning, knitting, and weaving. Their smaller size and relative ease of handling make dairy goats more city-friendly than cows. They are also social creatures and can help increase the bond between city residents and the food they consume.

While the idea might seem novel, goats have been an integral part of human settlements for thousands of years. Urban goat farming also presents a vivid example of 'zero-mileage' food, where the gap between the producer and the consumer bridges to near non-existence.

10.4. Navigating Goat Ownership in the City

When thinking about urban goat farming, the reality of space, feeding, and welfare logistics must be acknowledged. Housing goats would require enough space for them to move around, play, and exert sufficient energy. They need a varied diet, which is more challenging in a densely populated area with less grazing opportunity.

Moreover, goats need companionship, so keeping a single goat is not recommended. This need for peer interaction is one more aspect that ought to be factored in before plunging into urban goat farming. Similar to chicken farming, zoning laws frequently dictate the feasibility of urban goat keeping.

10.5. The Benefit of Bees and Other Insects

Moving away from what is traditionally viewed as 'livestock', bees are also a significant part of urban agriculture. They add an essential layer to the city farming ecosystem by pollinating plants and providing honey and wax. Plus, their presence has been shown to increase biodiversity in the urban environment.

10.6. Cultivating a City Hive

City dwellers, bedazzled by the buzzing promise of homegrown honey, have embraced beekeeping. But, it's not only about the sweet, golden nectar produced in a backyard beehive. There is a profound satisfaction in fostering a creature that plays such an important ecological role.

However, the maintenance of an urban hive brings its own unique challenges. The selection of apiary location must be done with care, taking into account factors such as flight paths, noise for neighbors, and access to food sources for the bees.

10.7. Wide Spectrum of Urban Livestock

While chickens, goats, and bees can be seen as the poster children of urban livestock, creative urban farmers have adapted to the metropolis's constraints by branching out to other species like rabbits, ducks, or quails. This diversification allows urban farmers to continually redefine the limitations and possibilities of this ever-evolving pursuit.

The world of urban livestock is a dynamic and innovative space. Through a mixture of creativity, resilience, and a deep respect for nature's bounty, city-dwellers are leading a quiet revolution. This revolution is transforming concrete jungles into verdant, productive lands infused with buzzing hives and clucking hens — or even the occasional bleat of a neighborhood goat.

The future of food is already being written into the ever-changing skyline, one rooftop farm, and backyard homestead at a time. Embracing the 'green in gray' stands as testament to our adaptability, resilience, and enduring aspiration toward sustainability.

Chapter 11. The Future of Urban Agriculture: Policies, Innovation, and Opportunities

Today's sprawling concrete jungles are not traditionally associated with sustainable agriculture. Yet as the world's population continues to surge, concerns regarding ecosystem degradation and food security have brought the spotlight onto urban farming. Beyond the immediate benefits of a greener environment and fresh, locally grown food, urban agriculture represents a revolution in sustainability, introducing innovative changes to traditional city policies and structures. As we delve into the future of urban agriculture, we gain a unique perspective on the myriad of policies, innovations, and opportunities that this new dawn brings for our cities.

11.1. Advancements in Urban Agriculture Practices and Innovations

Innovations in urban agricultural practices are a testament to humanity's artistic and innovative spirit. Drawing inspiration from natural ecosystems, these advancements mirror permaculture principles, integrating sustainability and design in an urban context.

Vertical farming optimizes limited space, creating multi-story greenhouses with features such as root misting and LED lighting. Such farms exponentially increase the available growing area without requiring additional land. Meanwhile, hydroponics and aeroponics eliminate the need for soil, enabling indoor farming closer to consumers and reducing dependency on remote food sources. Similarly, precision farming technologies, such as climate control systems and automated irrigation, further maximize yield while reducing input and waste.

As new technologies are assimilate into urban farming, transformative processes like 'recycling urban waste' are gaining traction. Kitchen scraps turned into compost, and wastewater treated and reused in urban farm plots, not only provide nutrients for plants but also alleviate urban waste management challenges. The concept of "circular economy" is becoming a design principle for cities, integrating waste management into urban agriculture and reducing ecological footprints.

11.2. Shaping Policy to Foster Urban Agriculture

As urban agriculture evolves, existing legal and regulatory frameworks must also adapt to foster rather than stifle development. Engaging various stakeholders, including policymakers, legislators, urban planners, and local communities, is key to implementing supportive policies.

Enlightened city planning can prioritize provision for urban farms in new development projects, ensuring reserved, productive green spaces. Building codes may be amended to enable rooftop greenhouses and basement aquaponics systems. Welfare programs can introduce incentives for low-income households to participate in urban farming activities, supporting local food production and security while providing income or sustenance. Agriculture and environmental regulations must be reframed to incorporate urban contexts without undermining existing safety and quality standards.

Beyond local policy, urban agriculture can influence national and international urban development policy. Intersecting realms of sustainability, health, and resilience, urban farming can shape conversations on climate change, biodiversity, and the right to food.

11.3. Unearthed Opportunities: Urban Agriculture's Promises

Urban agriculture is packed with the potential for socio-economic and environmental benefits. It provides a platform for urban residents to reconnect with nature, increasing awareness and appreciation of the delicate interdependencies within our food systems.

Job opportunities are created through the lifecycle of urban farm projects, from planning, building, and maintenance, to harvest, distribution, and waste management. Micro-economies can spring from successful urban farms, providing fresh, local produce, thus reducing food miles and improving access to nutritional food in food deserts.

Environmentally, integrating green spaces into the urban landscape aids air purification, heat island mitigation, and biodiversity. Additionally, urban farms with native plants can act as stepping stones for pollinators, promoting urban biodiversity.

==–Remaining Obstacles and Challenges

Despite the optimism, significant work remains. Institutional barriers, lack of funding or proper planning, and public misunderstanding or distrust must be overcome. Gaps in knowledge and skills need bridging through education and training. Eminent domain, gentrification, and land rights issues must be considered to ensure urban farming practices are fair and equitable. To truly realize the potential of urban agriculture, systemic change encompassing attitude, policy, and practice is required.

Urban agriculture is an adventure of exploration and reinvention, pushing boundaries of conventional practices towards a sustainable, resilient future. It is the confluence of science, practicality, and creativity, fostering a viable path in an improbable environment. It awakens a connection to the green heartbeat beneath the gray concrete, and invites all to participate. This journey is not without its challenges, yet it is through these trials we might find a new harmony between the urban and the organic, the gray and the green.